FOR MY PARENTS —N.D.

FOR WILL —C.R.T.

Random House Studio
An imprint of Random House Children's Books
A division of Penguin Random House LLC
1745 Broadway, New York, NY 10019
penguinrandomhouse.com
rhcbooks.com

Library of Congress Cataloging-in-Publication Data is available upon request.
ISBN 978-0-593-90569-2 (trade)—ISBN 978-0-593-90570-8 (lib. bdg.)—ISBN 978-0-593-90571-5 (ebook)

The text of this book is set in 14.5-point Quasimoda Semibold.
The illustrations were rendered in pencil, watercolor, colored pencil, and ink, assembled digitally.
Interior design by Rachael Cole

Manufactured in China
10 9 8 7 6 5 4 3 2 1

The authorized representative in the EU for product safety and compliance is Penguin Random House Ireland, Morrison Chambers, 32 Nassau Street, Dublin D02 YH68, Ireland, https://eu-contact.penguin.ie.

A RIDDLE OF EELS

WRITTEN BY NICHOLAS DAY
ILLUSTRATED BY COREY R. TABOR

RANDOM HOUSE STUDIO NEW YORK

poof

If you were an eel, all slimy and sleek, then . . .

. . . then that would be very helpful, actually.

Because then—and I know this is asking a lot, since you have just become an eel, which must be a shock—you could somehow pass along word of what it is like.

(I also know that would be difficult, since you'd be an eel and all, but do your best.)

Then I'd put it in a picture book, and we'd know all about eels.

That would be great.

glub
glub-glub
glub!

Now, maybe you were expecting that *this* book would tell you all about eels.

Most books are about things we already know, after all.

A book about sea otters tells you that sea otters carry around a favorite rock in their pouch.

A book about albatrosses tells you that albatrosses can fly for over a year without touching land.

A book about blue whales tells you that baby blues gain two hundred pounds a day.

So a book about eels ought to tell you about eels.

And I can tell you a few things about eels.

We know that there are eels all over the world, and that they've been around far longer than us, and that they're fish even though they look like snakes.

We know mostly what they eat (small fish, large insects),

mostly where they live (in the muck, in the shallows),

mostly when they hunt (in the dark, in the night).

We know that some eels, as if determined to stay in disguise, change their very form: They go from thin, glassy ribbons to long flashes of yellow to explosive silver coils.

Usually, the more we study something, the more we know about it.

This is how we know that sea otters have favorite rocks, and that albatrosses can stay aloft for so long, and that a baby blue whale eats the weight of a washing machine every single day.

The eel is different.

The more we study it, the *less* we know about it.

There is a famous quote by Winston Churchill, a man who once governed Great Britain and said a lot of things that became famous. This time, he called something difficult to understand *a riddle wrapped in a mystery inside an enigma.*

A riddle is a mystery, and an enigma is a mystery, so Churchill was saying that something difficult to understand was *a mystery wrapped in a mystery inside a mystery.*

But he could have saved all those words.
He could have just called that something *an eel.*
That's a real eel of a problem, he could have said.

For thousands of years, scientists, naturalists, philosophers—anyone with any sense of wonder—they all looked hard at the eel.

They observed it. They caught it. They cut it open.

They imagined—well, we do not know if they imagined they were an eel. We do not know if they said to themselves, *If I were an eel, all slimy and sleek—*

But I like to think they did. The eel is a magical creature. It casts a spell.

And after all this observing, and maybe even after all this imagining, they came to a few conclusions.

Aristotle, for example, a Greek philosopher, concluded that eels came from mud.

There can be no doubt about this being so, he wrote.

And so that was that.

Until someone else came along—let's say Pliny the Elder, a Roman naturalist—and concluded something entirely different.

Pliny concluded that *actually* eels came from eels scraping themselves against rocks.

Those little scrapings of eel sprang to life, Pliny wrote.

And so that was that.

Until someone else came along and concluded that *actually* eels came from the swirls of sea-foam,

or that *actually* eels came from the sun twinkling on the dew,

or that *actually* eels came from the hairs of the tails of horses.

There have been so many *actuallys*.

All this disagreeing went on for centuries, because eels are both bewitching and bewildering, and after a while, everyone managed to agree on this:

Eels are really easy to disagree about.

Eels are a real eel of a problem, you could say.

It is easy to see how people might disagree about the shadowy, rare giant squid. It's shadowy! It's rare!

It is easy to see how people might disagree about the terrifying, isolated Komodo dragon. It's terrifying! It's isolated!

It is less easy to see how people might disagree about the eel.

The eel is not rare. The eel is not terrifying. The eel is not isolated.

The eel is all around us.

For centuries, to stand at the mouth of some rivers when the eels arrived was to witness a swarm, a flood, a tidal wave of eelness.

More than a billion eels swam up the rivers of Europe *each year.*

To wet your hand in these waters was to touch an eel.

But the eel is hard to hold. It slips from our grasp.

We do not know how long eels can live, not really.

We do not know why and when they change their form, not really.

And for years, we did not know where eels came from.

No one had ever caught a baby eel. No one had ever *seen* a baby eel.

We did not know how eels made other eels. We did not even know *if* eels made other eels.

These are not supposed to be hard questions, you know. These are the most basic questions we ask about any living being.

And yet we were unable to answer these basic questions even though we were *surrounded by eels.*

Every time we came up with an answer, we'd learn something else and it was as if the eel itself was saying to us:

Actually.

glub*
*Actually.

There's a term for how much we don't know about the eel. It's called the Eel Question.

Originally, the question meant: *Where do eels come from?*

But maybe it also should mean: *After looking at something for so long, how can we know so little?*

Or maybe, maybe:

If a book about eels doesn't tell you about eels, then what does it tell you about?

Thousands of years after Aristotle, a man named Johannes Schmidt got on a ship.

He was going wherever eels came from. He just didn't know where that was.

And he didn't know if he'd ever get there.

For decades, Johannes Schmidt sailed around the Atlantic, catching eels.

Some of those eels were smaller and younger than other eels, and some eels were smaller and younger still, and some eels were even *smaller and younger*—and when, at last, Johannes Schmidt had found the smallest and youngest eel he could find, something not even recognizable as an eel, something the size and shape of a tiny leaf, he declared that *here* was the birthplace of the eel: the Sargasso Sea, a small swirl of the Atlantic.

There was a problem, however.
There was an *actually*.

Johannes Schmidt thought that every eel that swam up the rivers of Europe and North America was born in the Sargasso Sea. And he thought that every eel, at the end of its long life, swam back there to make more eels.

That meant there were millions of eels migrating each year to the Sargasso Sea.

And yet Johannes Schmidt had not found—*he could not find*—a single full-grown eel there. He'd only found these wisps, these ghosts of eel future.

He'd spent his life following the eel.
And yet it had remained *a riddle*
wrapped in a mystery inside an enigma.

It is now a century after Johannes Schmidt stepped off his ship for the final time.

We have still never seen a full-grown eel in the Sargasso Sea.

But we are as sure as we can be that they are born in this patch of profound blue. And at the end of their lives, they return.

The way home measures thousands of miles. It takes some eels half a year to make the trip. They do so without eating. They do so without a map.

It is among the most extraordinary journeys made by any living being.

We don't know if they are guided by some sort of internal compass. We don't know if they are guided by the light of the moon. We don't know if they are guided by smell. We don't know if they are guided by feel.

We don't know.

A book about eels ought to tell you about eels.

If a book about eels doesn't tell you about eels, then what does it tell you about?

We know so much about our world. It's blinding, how much we know. It makes it hard to see how much we *don't* know.

But sometimes there's a crack in our wall of knowledge.

And through it, we can catch a glimpse of the vast, wondrous world that's still unknown to us.

And we can watch as a riddle of eels swims, serenely, through that crack.

And out of sight.

If you were an eel, all slimy and sleek, then—

—well, then good luck out there, kid.

SOMETHING ELSE WE KNOW ABOUT EELS

There are fewer all the time.

The world is wild with eels. There are almost a thousand species, but this book focuses on the American and European sort—the same eel, really. (They're impossible to tell apart if you don't count the vertebrae, and even then, sometimes you can't tell.) The eels are born and they die in the golden seaweed of the Sargasso Sea. For the rest of their lives, the two species are separated by the Atlantic—the American eels having left the Sargasso to swim up the rivers of the Americas, the Europeans to swim up the rivers of Europe—but they are still suffering the same dwindling fate.

The population of the American eel has crashed, bottoming out at a historically low level. The European eel is critically endangered. The eels arrive on the coasts each year in numbers a tiny fraction of what they once were. Where there were twenty, now there is only one—a stunning 95 percent decline.

Why is a good question, and there are too many answers. There's overfishing, especially when eels are newly arrived from the Sargasso and still slight and glassy. There are the dried-up wetlands, the polluted rivers and lakes. There are the dams on rivers, stopping the eels on their journey upstream, sometimes slicing up those that attempt it anyway. And then there's climate change, which is already changing everything about the environment of the eel—including the very currents it floats on.

The eel is slipping out of its own story.

We have spent centuries—millennia—trying to understand the eel. Because it was—it is—a wonder. Because we were—we are—curious.

But now we are also trying to understand the eel so that we can *save* it.

And how do you save a creature you scarcely know?

Scientists have attached satellite tags to eels, and those eels have ended up in the Sargasso Sea—but the scientists have still never seen the eels there. In the slippery world of eel research, this satellite evidence has proved, at long last, what Johannes Schmidt proposed a century ago: The Sargasso is the wellspring of eels.

We know far more than Schmidt, vastly more, but the darkness is still deep.

We don't know what prompts eels to leave their rivers and return to the ocean. We don't know how they find their way. We don't know how eels ended up making this extraordinary, preposterous migration—

a journey that lingers on the far side of the possible.

The eel is a flash in the water, less a fish than a specter.

It is tempting to say that we need to know not for our sake, but for *theirs*.

It would be wrong, though. Because a world without eels—without its annual surge of eelness—would be a smaller, poorer world for *us*.

The great environmentalist Rachel Carson was enamored with eels. She once explained why.

"To see an eel," Carson wrote over eighty years ago, "is something like meeting a person who has traveled to the most remote and wonderful places of the earth; in a flash I see a vivid picture of the strange places that eel has been—places which I, being merely human, can never visit."

SOURCES

Carson, Rachel. *Lost Woods: The Discovered Writing of Rachel Carson*. Edited by Linda Lear. Beacon Press, 1998.

Carson, Rachel. *Under the Sea-Wind*. Penguin, 2007. Originally published in 1941 by Simon & Schuster.

Prosek, James. *Eels: An Exploration, from New Zealand to the Sargasso, of the World's Most Mysterious Fish*. Harper, 2010.

Svensson, Patrik. *The Book of Eels: Our Enduring Fascination with the Most Mysterious Creature in the Natural World*. Ecco, 2020.

Williams, Paige. "Inside the Slimy, Smelly, Secretive World of Glass-Eel Fishing." *The New Yorker*, June 17, 2024.

Wright, Rosalind M., Adam T. Piper, Kim Aarestrup, et al. "First Direct Evidence of Adult European Eels Migrating to Their Breeding Place in the Sargasso Sea." *Scientific Reports* 12, no. 1 (October 13, 2022).